Searchlight BOOKS

What
Is a
Food Web?

Tundra Food Webs

in Action

Paul Fleisher

Lerner Publications Company
Minneapolis

Lerner Publications Company
A division of Lerner Publishing Group, Inc.
241 First Avenue North
Minneapolis, MN 55401 U.S.A.

Website address: www.lernerbooks.com

Library of Congress Cataloging-in-Publication Data

Fleisher, Paul.
    Tundra food webs in action / by Paul Fleisher.
        p.   cm. — (Searchlight books™—What is a food web?)
    Includes index.
    ISBN 978-1-4677-1295-8 (lib. bdg. : alk. paper)
    ISBN 978-1-4677-1778-6 (eBook)
    1. Tundra ecology—Juvenile literature. 2. Food chains (Ecology)—Juvenile literature. I. Title.
    QH541.5.T8F54 2014
    577.5'86—dc23   2012034178

Manufactured in the United States of America
1 – BP – 7/15/13

Contents

A TUNDRA FOOD WEB

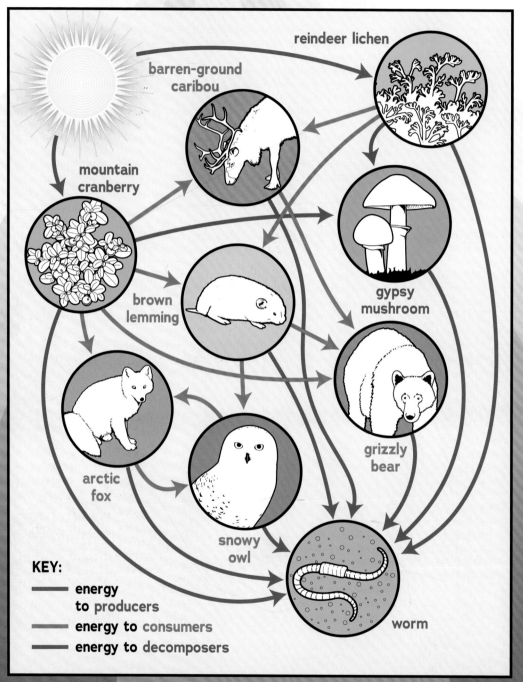

reindeer lichen

barren-ground caribou

mountain cranberry

brown lemming

gypsy mushroom

arctic fox

grizzly bear

snowy owl

worm

KEY:
— energy to producers
— energy to consumers
— energy to decomposers

Chapter 1

THE TUNDRA

The land of the far north is called the tundra. It is a harsh place to live. Most of the tundra is flat. No trees grow there. The air is dry. Strong winds blow.

Winters are long and cold in the tundra. The ground is frozen. It is covered with snow. Some days, the sun never rises.

The sun sets over the tundra in the winter. What is the tundra like during the winter?

5

Summer

Tundra summers are short. They last only a couple of months. During the summer, the sun shines brightly. On some days, the sun never sets.

Each summer, the tundra buzzes with life. Flowers bloom. Birds raise their young. Insects fill the air.

COLORFUL WILDFLOWERS
BLOOM IN A TUNDRA MEADOW.

In the summer, the top layer of soil thaws. That part of the ground is called the active layer. Plants and animals can live in the active layer.

Below the active layer, the ground stays frozen. The frozen layer is called permafrost. Permafrost is very deep.

Melting snow and ice form pools of water on the tundra. Some of the water drains into a nearby river.

Snow, Water, and Ice

In the summer, the snow melts. Water seeps into the active layer. But water cannot soak into the permafrost. The water has no place to go. So the surface of the tundra stays wet. Marshes and ponds form.

Each winter, the water freezes again. When water freezes, it expands. Ice pushes in all directions. Ice pushes up round hills called pingos. The ice also forms cracks across the land. From above, the tundra looks like a jigsaw puzzle.

A pingo forms when water freezes underground. When ice pushes up on the land, a hill forms.

Environment

The tundra is an important environment. An environment is the place where any creature lives. The environment includes the air, soil, and weather. It includes other plants and animals too.

TUNDRA AREAS OF EARTH

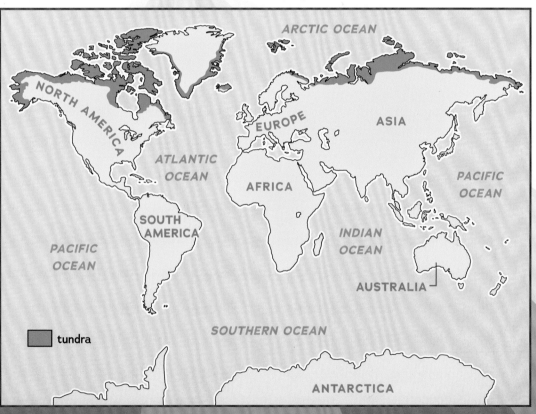

ARCTIC OCEAN

NORTH AMERICA

EUROPE

ASIA

ATLANTIC OCEAN

AFRICA

PACIFIC OCEAN

SOUTH AMERICA

INDIAN OCEAN

PACIFIC OCEAN

AUSTRALIA

☐ tundra

SOUTHERN OCEAN

ANTARCTICA

About one-twentieth of Earth's land is tundra. There is tundra in Alaska. Tundra stretches across northern Canada. Northern Europe and Asia are covered with tundra too.

Living things on the tundra depend on one another. Some animals eat plants. Many animals eat other animals. Some creatures feed on plants and animals that have died. When plants and animals die, they break down into chemicals. The chemicals become part of the soil. Some of these chemicals help plants grow.

ANTLERS AND OTHER ANIMAL BONES SLOWLY BREAK DOWN. THEY BECOME PART OF THE TUNDRA'S SOIL. NEW PLANTS GROW IN THE SOIL.

Food Chains

Energy moves from one living thing to another. A food chain shows how living things get energy. Energy for life comes from the sun. Plants store the sun's energy in their leaves, stems, and roots. Animals eat the plants. They get some of the sun's energy from the plants. The energy moves along the food chain. When one creature eats another, some of the energy is passed on.

The sun shines on a moose as it eats a willow plant. The moose gets some of the sun's energy from the willow.

A collared lemming eats part of a dwarf willow in its burrow in the active layer.

The tundra has many food chains. Here is one example. A willow plant gets energy from the sun. A lemming eats the leaves and stems of the willow. Then a fox eats the lemming. Later, the fox dies. Tiny living things called bacteria feed on its body.

The sun's energy goes from the plant to the lemming. Then some of the energy goes to the fox. Then some of the energy goes to the bacteria.

Lemmings do not eat only willow plants. They also eat lichens and berries. Foxes eat other things besides lemmings. Foxes eat birds, eggs, and berries. Bacteria feed on all kinds of dead animals and plants. The tundra's many food chains make up a food web. A food web shows how all living things in an environment depend on one another for food.

An arctic fox pounces on a small animal moving under the snow.

Chapter 2

TUNDRA PLANTS

Green plants use sunlight to make food. Living things that make their own food from sunlight are called producers. Plants also make oxygen. Oxygen is a gas in the air. All animals need oxygen to breathe.

The tundra's energy comes from the sun. Northern primrose and other tundra plants use sunlight to make food. What else do plants make?

Making Food and Oxygen

Plants make food and oxygen through photosynthesis. Plants need carbon dioxide, sunlight, and water for photosynthesis. Carbon dioxide is a gas in the air. Plant leaves take in carbon dioxide and sunlight. The roots take in water. Plants use energy from the sunlight to turn the carbon dioxide and water into sugar and starch. Plants store this food in their leaves and roots.

HOW PHOTOSYNTHESIS WORKS

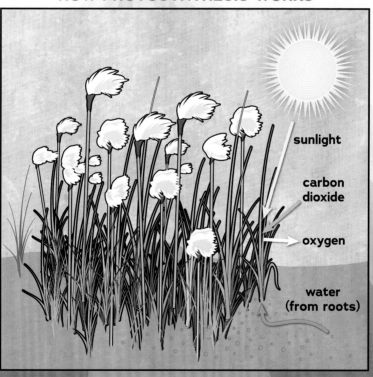

sunlight

carbon dioxide

oxygen

water (from roots)

Cotton grass turns sunlight, carbon dioxide, and water into food for itself.

When plants make food, they also make oxygen. The oxygen goes into the air. Animals breathe in oxygen. They breathe out carbon dioxide. Plants use the carbon dioxide to make more food.

Plants grow in soil. The soil contains chemicals called nutrients. Living things need nutrients to grow. Water soaks into the soil. Nutrients from the soil go into the water. The plants' roots take in the water and get nutrients from the soil. The nutrients become part of each plant.

The roots of tundra plants take in water from the active layer. The water comes from melted ice and snow.

Seasons on the Tundra

On the tundra, there is little sunshine in the winter. Snow falls and stays on the ground. But plants live under the snow. They have stored the food they made in the summer. Animals depend on the energy stored in those plants.

AN ARCTIC GROUND SQUIRREL EATS SEEDS FROM GRASS THAT IS COVERED BY SNOW.

Crowberry plants grow fruit that animals eat.

Tundra plants grow for only about two months each year. Their roots can grow only in the active layer. Plants cannot send roots into the permafrost. So the plants grow in the summer, when the active layer is unfrozen.

In the summer, the tundra is covered with colorful plants. Flowers bloom. Many tundra plants have berries. Cranberries and blueberries make good food for animals.

Sedges also grow on the tundra. Sedges look like grass. Cotton grass is a sedge that grows in thick clumps. It grows in drier parts of the tundra. Sedges also grow in wet areas. Moss grows in the marshes too.

Reindeer lichen grows on the tundra all year. Lichens are algae and fungi growing together. Animals eat lichens in the winter.

Lichens are plantlike living things. Reindeer lichens are important producers on the tundra.

Chapter 3

TUNDRA PLANT EATERS

Living things that eat other living things are consumers. *Consume* means "eat." Animals are consumers. Animals that eat plants are called herbivores. The sun's energy is stored in the plants. When an animal eats a plant, it gets the sun's energy.

A caribou eats grass after a snowfall. What other tundra animals eat plants?

Many tundra insects feed on plants. During the summer, insects eat leaves and roots. Bumblebees fly from flower to flower. They drink from the flowers. Other insects live in ponds. They eat plants growing in the water.

A bumblebee rests on the flower of a fireweed.

Birds

Many birds migrate to the tundra each summer. They travel there to find plants to eat. Millions of geese fly to the tundra. Swans and ducks go there too. They eat pond plants and grasses. They make nests and raise their young.

Ptarmigans live on the tundra all year. These birds are much like chickens. In the winter, ptarmigans scratch away snow to find food. They eat seeds and berries. Ptarmigans grow white feathers each winter. The white color helps them hide in the snow. They hide from other tundra animals.

Rock ptarmigans have white feathers in the winter and brown feathers in the summer.

Mammals

The fur of some tundra mammals turns white in the winter. Arctic hares are white. In the summer, some arctic hares grow brown fur.

Lemmings stay busy all year. They tunnel under the snow. They search for seeds and berries. They eat plant stems and roots. Voles look like mice. Voles tunnel under the snow all winter too. They search for plants to eat.

An arctic hare nibbles on a plant in the winter. Arctic hares eat the leaves and stems of tundra plants.

Musk oxen's thick hair helps them stay warm during tundra winters.

Musk oxen are the largest herbivores on the tundra. They live there all year. Musk oxen kick snow away with their hooves. The oxen eat the plants underneath the snow.

In the summer, moose, elk, and caribou come to feed on tundra plants. Caribou travel in large herds. They eat willows and sedges in the summer. Each winter, most caribou travel south. They migrate to find more food. A few stay on the tundra all winter. They eat lichens.

Chapter 4

TUNDRA MEAT EATERS

Carnivores are animals that eat meat. They catch and eat other animals. But carnivores depend on plants too. Carnivores get energy from eating animals that have eaten plants.

A horned lark has caught an insect to eat. What are animals that eat other animals called?

Many biting insects live in the tundra. Mosquitoes are carnivores. They feed on the blood of birds and mammals. Gnats and flies also feed on blood.

Fish swim in the rivers and lakes. A kind of fish called arctic char eats insects. It also eats other small animals. So do grayling and whitefish.

Mosquitoes are feeding on the blood of this loon.

Birds and Wolves

Some tundra birds are carnivores. Snowy owls hunt lemmings and voles. In the summer, millions of other birds migrate to the tundra to find animals to eat. Baby birds feast on insects. Falcons and cranes hunt for other birds. Cranes also eat fish and small mammals. So do eagles.

Wolves catch many animals in the summertime. Wolves travel in packs. They hunt small mammals and birds. Wolves kill and eat caribou too.

A pack of gray wolves eat an animal that they killed.

Omnivores

Some animals eat both plants and animals. These animals are called omnivores. Arctic foxes are omnivores. Foxes eat many different things. They catch lemmings and voles. Foxes also eat birds and eggs. But foxes eat berries too.

Grizzly bears are omnivores. They eat small mammals. These bears hunt caribou and catch fish. Grizzly bears also eat fruit and berries.

Grizzly bears migrate to the tundra in the summer to find food. This grizzly bear found some soapberries to eat.

Chapter 5

TUNDRA DECOMPOSERS

All living things die. When
plants or animals die, they decay.
They break down into nutrients.
Living things called decomposers help
dead things decay. Decomposers feed on
dead creatures.

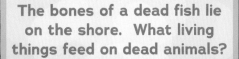

The bones of a dead fish lie
on the shore. What living
things feed on dead animals?

Nature's Recyclers

Decomposers are nature's recyclers. They break down dead plants and animals. Nutrients from the dead things go back into the soil. Other living things can use those nutrients to grow. Without decomposers, dead plants and animals would cover the tundra. Then no new plants could grow. Animals would run out of food.

Tiny decomposers are feeding on the body of this reindeer. They are breaking it down into nutrients.

Decomposers will feed slowly on these remains of a musk ox. It could take many years for them to break down the body.

Dead creatures decay slowly on the tundra. For most of the year, everything is frozen. It is too cold for things to decay. Nutrients do not go back into the soil quickly. So tundra soil has few nutrients. That is another reason why tundra plants grow slowly.

Scavengers

Some tundra animals are scavengers. They find and eat the meat of dead animals. Ravens are scavengers. These birds look for animals that have died. Foxes follow large carnivores. The large carnivores hunt and kill other animals to eat. Later, foxes eat what is left.

Worms feed on dead plants and animals. They help the dead creatures rot away. So do insects such as beetles and flies. Some insects feed on droppings from animals.

This pile of droppings contains berries and other food that a bear ate. Young flies and beetles will feed on the droppings.

Mushrooms and Bacteria

Mushrooms and other fungi are decomposers. They grow during the wet summer season. They feed on dead plants.

Bacteria are the most important decomposers. They are so tiny we cannot see them. Bacteria feed on all kinds of dead plants and animals.

MUSHROOMS GROW IN TUNDRA PEAT MOSS.

Chapter 6

PEOPLE AND THE TUNDRA

Few people live on the tundra. It is too cold. There are no large cities. There are no farms.

But some people do live on the tundra. Some native people live by hunting and fishing. Others have moved to towns.

This woman is ice fishing near a village in Alaska. Do many people live on the tundra?

In Europe and Asia, some people herd reindeer. Reindeer are a kind of caribou. People living on the tundra eat reindeer meat. They make clothing from reindeer skin. Some people work on the tundra. They hunt. They also trap animals for fur. But they have to be careful not to kill too many animals.

Years ago, hunters killed almost all the musk oxen in North America. People had to stop hunting them. More musk oxen live in Canada and Alaska again.

Mining and Drilling

Some parts of the tundra have valuable metals under the ground. There is also oil deep underground. People work in mines to get metals. Others work on oil wells.

People must be careful when they mine or drill in the tundra. Oil drilling uses heavy machines. So does mining. The machines can damage the tundra. And oil spills kill plants and animals. Tundra plants grow slowly. If they are damaged, the plants take many years to grow back.

The trans-Alaska pipeline carries oil across Alaska. The pipes were built above the ground on the tundra. That way, the oil does not melt the permafrost.

Climate

The greatest danger to the tundra is Earth's changing climate. The world is slowly getting warmer. More tundra ice melts each year. Tundra plants and animals need the cold to live. As the tundra gets warmer, they may die out or move away. Other creatures may take their place.

The tundra is a very special place. Many creatures that live there live nowhere else. We must take care of the tundra.

Polar bears live only in the far north. They hunt animals that live in or near the Arctic Ocean. But warm temperatures are melting the ice where they hunt.

Glossary

active layer: the top layer of tundra soil that thaws each summer. Plants and animals live in this layer.

bacteria: tiny living things made of just one cell. Bacteria can be seen only under a microscope.

carnivore: an animal that eats meat

consumer: a living thing that eats other living things. Animals are consumers.

decay: to break down

decomposer: a living thing that feeds on dead plants and animals and breaks them down into nutrients

environment: a place where a creature lives. An environment includes the air, soil, weather, plants, and animals in a place.

food chain: the way energy moves from the sun to a plant, then to a plant eater, then to a meat eater, and finally to a decomposer

food web: many food chains connected together. A food web shows how all living things in a place need one another for food.

herbivore: an animal that eats plants

lichen: a plantlike living thing that is part algae and part fungi

mammal: an animal that feeds its babies milk and has hair on its body

nutrient: a chemical that living things need to grow

omnivore: an animal that eats both plants and animals

permafrost: the layer of soil under the tundra that stays frozen all year

photosynthesis: the way green plants use energy from sunlight to make their own food from carbon dioxide and water

producer: a living thing that makes its own food. Plants are producers.

Learn More about the Tundra and Food Webs

Books

Latham, Donna. *Tundra*. White River Junction, VT: Nomad Press, 2010. Investigate the tundra to see how its landscape and living things exist in harmony.

Levy, Janey. *Discovering the Arctic Tundra*. New York: PowerKids Press, 2008. Learn more about the climate, plants, animals, and people of the cold, windy tundra, and find out why the tundra is important.

Wojahn, Rebecca Hogue, and Donald Wojahn. *A Tundra Food Chain: A Who-Eats-What Adventure in the Arctic*. Minneapolis: Lerner Publications Company, 2009. What you choose to eat shapes your fate in this fun, interactive story about food chains.

Websites

Chain Reaction
http://www.ecokids.ca/pub/eco_info/topics/frogs/chain_reaction
Create a food chain and find out what happens if you take one link out of the chain.

Enchanted Learning: Tundra Animal Printouts
http://www.enchantedlearning.com/biomes/tundra/tundra.shtml
Click on a tundra animal to learn what it looks like and what it eats.

Kids Do Ecology: Tundra
http://kids.nceas.ucsb.edu/biomes/tundra.html
Read all about the weather, plants, and animals of Earth's coldest biome and play games to explore your new knowledge.

LERNER
e
SOURCE

Expand learning beyond the printed book. Download free, complementary educational resources for this book from our website, www.lerneresource.com.

Index

Photo Acknowledgments

The images in this book are used with the permission of: Zeke Smith, pp. 4, 15; © iStockphoto.com/ArildHeitmann, p. 5; © Jupiterimages/Photos.com/Thinkstock, p. 6; © Gary Schultz, pp. 7, 8, 14, 16, 17, 26, 31; © Laura Westlund/Independent Picture Service, p. 9; © Denis Trofimov/Dreamstime.com, p. 10; © Danita Delimont/Gallo Images/Getty Images, p. 11; © Biosphoto/Photo Researchers, Inc., p. 12; © Steven Kazlowski/Science Faction/SuperStock, pp. 13, 34; © Dmitry Knorre/Dreamstime.com, p. 18; © Aleksandrn/Dreamstime.com, p. 19; © iStockphoto.com/Geoff Kuchera, p. 20; © Oksix/Dreamstime.com, p. 21; © Tom Walker/Visuals Unlimited, Inc., p. 22 (left); © Maximilian Buzun/Dreamstime.com, p. 22 (right); © age fotostock/SuperStock, p. 23; © NHPA/SuperStock, p. 24; © Patrick J. Endres/Visuals Unlimited, Inc., pp. 25, 27; © Minden Pictures/SuperStock, p. 28; © Prisma/SuperStock, p. 29; © iStockphoto.com/Laila Røberg, p. 30; © Fritz Polking/Visuals Unlimited, Inc., p. 32; © Alan Majchrowicz/Peter Arnold/Getty Images, p. 33; © Mark Hamblin/Oxford Scientific/Getty Images, p. 35; © Sam Chadwick/Shutterstock.com, p. 36; © GeoStock/Photodisc/Getty Images, p. 37. Front Cover: © iStockphoto.com/Liz Leyden.

Main body text set in Adrianna Regular 14/20.
Typeface provided by Chank.